JANUA LINGUARUM

STUDIA MEMORIAE
NICOLAI VAN WIJK DEDICATA

edenda curat
C. H. VAN SCHOONEVELD

Indiana University

Series Practica, 162

THE PHONETICS
OF
MODERN HEBREW

by

M. J. CHAYEN

The Hebrew University, Jerusalem

1973
MOUTON
THE HAGUE · PARIS

LIBRARY OF CONGRESS CATALOG CARD NUMBER: 72-88208

Printed in Hungary

PREFACE

This study originated as the first part of my "Investigation of the Phonology of Modern Hebrew", a dissertation prepared at the Massachusetts Institute of Technology and in Israel and for which a doctorate was awarded by the University of London in 1969. The original thesis was in two parts: Part I, a description of the "Phonetics of Colloquial Educated Israeli Hebrew" (E.I.H.) and Part II, a generative "Phonology" of the Hebrew described in Part I. Since the second Part, the generative phonology, is still undergoing computer verification, it was decided to postpone publication of that part of the work, until the required modifications and re-checking can be completed.

The "Phonetics" is the result of the analysis of the pronunciation of 29 native speakers recorded on tape in informal discussion. Although these recordings were made in 1967 and the findings written in 1968, I have since then, between 1969 and 1971, had the opportunity of recording the speech of over a hundred additional subjects. The analysis of this later body of data has fully confirmed the conclusions arrived at on the basis of the examination of the original group.

Consequently, and in view of the fact that the occasional articles so far published on Hebrew phonetics have been based on the speech of no more than only three or four speakers, it seemed pointless to delay publication of the "Phonetics" until such time as the "Phonology" of Part II could be finally verified, and this work therefore appears now as a separate and independent monograph.

The phonetic description presented here is purely articulatory in the tradition of Daniel Jones, in whose Department at University College, London, I was privileged to have studied in the years immediately prior to World War II. My debt of gratitude to Noam Chomsky and Morris Halle for their influence on the whole of my "Investigation", I intend to acknowledge more adequately in the forthcoming "Phonology". At this opportunity I should like to express appreciation and acknowledge the lasting influence of my early teachers at the department of Phonetics at University College, first Jean-Paul Vinay, now at Victoria, British Columbia, and later A. C. Gimson, now Professor of Phonetics at University College.

I wish to thank colleagues at the Hebrew University, particularly Chaim Blanc and Chaim Rabin, for having read the original draft of this work and Sholomo Morag for having indicated at the outset of the research some particular areas of

Hebrew phonetics which required clarifying. While recognizing the benefit I have had of their unequalled experience of the Hebrew language, I absolve them from all responsibility for any inaccuracies in my descriptions and conclusions.

I was able to amass my material only thanks to Professor Kaddari of Bar-Ilan University, Ramat-Gan, who showed interest in the project from the start and enabled me to make recordings of students in his Department of Hebrew and Semitic Languages.

The "Investigation" as a whole was encouraged by receipt of a Fullbright Travel Grant from the U.S. Education Foundation under the administration of Mr. Daniel Krauskopf.

M. J. CHAYEN
Jerusalem, May 1971

CONTENTS

0. INTRODUCTION

0.1. DEVELOPMENT OF MODERN HEBREW

Although Hebrew was the native language of Jews born in Palestine before 1948, native speakers formed a minority of the total Jewish population which in that year was 650,000[1] of whom the majority were immigrants, mostly from European countries. Three years after the establishment of the State of Israel, in May 1948, the population had doubled itself, this time due to an influx from Eastern, mainly Arabic speaking countries. By 1960 the population had tripled itself, a large variety of languages being spoken.

0.2. LINGUISTIC STABILITY ATTAINED SINCE 1960

Since the beginning of the last decade, the population of Israel seems, for the first time, to have reached a certain stability. As a result, the children today between the ages of five and seven have attended compulsory kindergarten in Israel, the fourteen year olds will have had eight years primary schooling in Israel, and students entering University will have completed four years at an Israeli secondary school having had at least four years in the country at primary school. So that today, at the beginning of the '70's, we may state as a general rule that all first year university students have been exposed to Hebrew as language of instruction at school as well as for every-day use since at least the age of eight. All those who have immigrated five years before the beginning of the last decade (before 1955) will have spoken Hebrew from kindergarten on, and are thus sufficient to be classified as native speakers.

0.3. MATERIAL ONLY NOW SUFFICIENTLY CONSOLIDATED TO WARRANT STUDY

The above statistical considerations suggest that it is fair to assume that spoken Israeli Hebrew has only now reached a state of consolidation which is sufficient to warrant its study as a natural native language of the Israeli community.

[1] Bachi 1956, 179–247.

0.4. CLASSICAL STUDIES WHICH OBSCURE FACTS OF SPOKEN LANGUAGE

Previous studies of Hebrew, as pointed out by Chaim Blanc[2], have done a lot to obscure the facts of the spoken language, "partly due to the rudimentary character of the research and partly to the polemical nature of the discussion", but probably mainly because the classical authorities in the field of Hebrew and Semitic languages were, of course, concerned with the classical language, and, in so far as they dealt with its spoken aspect, were forced to rely on old texts no longer subject to immediate audial examination.

0.5. HAMPERING OF FIELD WORK BY OVER – LITERATE INFORMANTS

From the beginning of the century it has been the professional schoolteacher who must be credited with the revival of Hebrew as the spoken language of Israel, but who, still today, prescribes a grammar and pronunciation in accordance with classical models, to his pupils, who have produced a new grammar and pronunciation of their own. No wonder then that the more scholarly the investigator the greater the degree in which he is influenced by his convictions about how the language should be shaped, or that even the young student or literate informant will tend to analyze his own speech in terms of the classical text book rather than on the basis of his own articulation.

[2] Blanc 1964.

1. THE TEXT

1.1. SUBJECTS RECORDED AND DATE

The text which provides the material for this description consists of taped recordings of the speech of undergraduates in informal conversations. In addition about half an hour of radio news broadcasts was recorded by two regular Kol Israel radio announcers. These recordings were all made in the first few months of 1967. Later in June 1967, a recording was added of General Rabin at his first press conference after the Six-Day War, his diction being particularly clear and his pronunciation typical of the type of native Hebrew of the third generation, which we shall call 'Educated Israeli Hebrew' (E.I.H.).

1.2. COUNTRIES OF ORIGIN OF INFORMANTS

The students recorded were not selected in any way. A complete class of 34 students studying Hebrew and Semitic Languages was recorded. The composition of the class was as follows: two students, aged over 40, whose schooling (primary and secondary) had been in Poland and Hungary respectively and whose Hebrew was patently coloured by their native languages; three Arab students, born and educated in Arab areas of Israel, whose Hebrew was unmistakably Arabic coloured. Of the remaining 29, 15 were born and educated in Israel, 14 were born outside Israel (in Persia, Czechoslovakia, the Yemen, Iraq, Rumania, Hungary, Cyprus, Germany, Poland, Lybia, Switzerland, Morocco, Tunisia, Russia), but most of these had attended nursery school already in Israel.

1.3. EDUCATED ISRAELI HEBREW (E. I. H.)

The speech of the 29 presents a homogeneity which warrants the study of the present corpus under the name of 'Educated Israeli Hebrew' (E.I.H.).[1]

---

[1] Blanc (1964:135) divides native Israeli Hebrew into "General Israeli" and "Arabicized Israeli", the latter spoken by Israelis of Eastern origin. "Educated Israeli" seems to be identical with Blanc's "General Israeli". The present recordings (1968) also bear out Blanc's assertion (1964) that there is no marked regional differentiation. Our recordings are of the same type of Hebrew, recorded as text by E. Levenston, and called "educated, colloquial, informal" (Levenston 1965).

2. THE VOWELS OF HEBREW

2.1. BASIS OF CLASSIFICATION

Our classification and description of the sounds of Hebrew speech will be in articulatory terms and will fall essentially within the two classes of vowels and consonants, these being understood in phonetic terms.[1] Following Halle[2] the articulation of all phones is to be classified as belonging to one of five degrees of constriction or narrowing of the vocal tract:

Degree 1: Greatest constriction, that is complete closure such as produces stops;
Degree 2: such as to produce turbulence, as in fricatives;
Degree 3: such as to produce semi-vowels and liquids;
Degree 4: such as to produce the close vowel types [i] [ɪ] [u] [ʊ];
Degree 5: negligible narrowing or fully open tract.

Consonants will therefore be those sounds produced with degree 1 or 2 of narrowing, and vowels will be sounds produced with degree 4 or 5 of narrowing. Between these two opposite classes degree 3 will comprise semi-vowels, glides and liquids, which both phonetically and linguistically partake of the nature of both vocalic and consonantal elements.

2.2. GENERAL FEATURES OF THE VOWELS

Hebrew (E.I.H.) has five[3] vowel segments, which may be represented by the IPA symbols: /i/, /e/, /a/, /o/ and /u/.

---

[1] Gimson's "vowel type" and "consonantal type" (Gimson 1962:28–29).

[2] Morris Halle, from lectures given in his course "Problems in Phonology" at the Massachusetts Institute of Technology, 1963–1964.

[3] Prof. Shelomo Morag (in private communication) claims a sixth vowel phoneme—a low back /a/ as evidenced by /nataGti/ 'I planted', as against /natati/ 'I gave'. This seems to be another example of the influence of literacy on phonetic judgement. An *ayin*—a back (grave) consonant—appears in the spelling, and even if not fully articulated may influence a learned pronunciation of the preceding /a/ vowel.

Hebrew has also a *shwa* (ə), a characteristically unstressed transition[4] vowel.

All vowels are non-nasal and voiced. The feature of length or tenseness is not linguistically significant.[5]

2.3. TONGUE POSITION OF THE VOWELS

A representation of the tongue position for each of the vowels is given in Diagram 1.

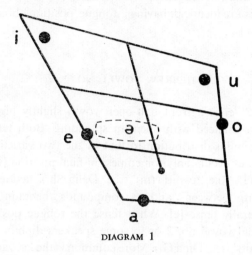

DIAGRAM 1

Only the back vowels /o/ and /u/ are rounded.

2.4. HEBREW VOWEL NO. 1 /i/

Hebrew vowel no. 1 /i/ has two main allophones, a tenser [i] and a laxer [ɪ]. The tenser member is a high front vowel pronounced with spread lips and appears most commonly in word-final position, e.g., /šeni/ 'second' /ani/ 'I' (rec. Oded B.[6]), /oti/ 'me'; /nimšaxti/ 'I continued' (rec. Aviva S.). Also in open stressed syllable final position, e.g., /ha′ji-ti/ 'I was', /ma′ci-a/ 'I suggest' (rec. Esther O.). Although tense, this vowel is slightly lower and less forward than Cardinal vowel no. 1, and less tense than French /i/ in, say, /fini/. More common is the laxer variety, which in some speakers is almost as low and retracted from the fully forward position as in the English lax /ɪ/ as in /bɪt/. Examples: the plural morpheme /-im/ as in /anašim/ 'people', /dvarim/

---

[4] Catford (no date) refers to the English neutral vowel as "not a vowel, but merely a momentary gap, or transition, between consonants". He therefore calls it a "transition".

[5] Prof. Chaim Rabin (in private communication) suggests that [ka : n] (spelled *kaʔn*) 'here' contrasts with [kan] (spelled *qan*) 'nest of'. This length distinction was not borne out by our informants.

[6] "rec." refers to the recordings in the Appendix.

'things' (rec. Sh. G.), also /tikva/ 'hope', /šivim/ 'seventy', (both vowels are [ɪ]) (rec. David Sh.).

Nevertheless the degree of laxity varies with the speaker, many having a marked tendency towards tenseness. This 'laxer tending to tense' quality of the /i/ vowel can best be appreciated in the pronunciation of the two borrowings from the English /ǧip/ 'jeep' and /čips/ 'chips'. A native English listener would hear the former as [ǧɪp] as in the English word 'gyp' or 'gipsy', with a lax vowel and the latter as [čips] or even [či:ps], as in the English 'cheap' with a tense vowel. In fact the two Hebrew vowels in these words are identical, having a tongue position about halfway between the two English vowels.

2.5. HEBREW VOWEL NO. 2 /e/

Hebrew vowel no. 2 /e/ is a front half-open vowel slightly higher than Cardinal vowel No. 3 [ɛ], pronounced with open lip spreading. Both tense [e] and lax [ɛ] varieties exist with similar distribution to that of the two varieties of /i/. However the tense variety of /e/ occurs only sometimes[7] in final position (word or morpheme final). Examples: /šte/, /šne/ 'two (f) (m)' (rec. Dalia Sh.), /axare/ 'after' (rec. Dina G.). The word /ben/ 'between', and its compounds /bentaim/ 'meanwhile' (rec. Dina G.) have generally tense [e]. When tense the tongue position of this vowel moves up to Cardinal vowel no. 2 or in some speakers diphthongizes to [ei], e.g., /horei-nu/ 'our parents' (rec. Dina G.). More common is the lax variety [ɛ]. Examples: /betsefer/ 'school', /ken/ 'yes' (rec. Dina G.); all with lax [ɛ], /ješ/ 'there is', /oved et 'she works' (rec. Zelda G.). This [ɛ] is found also in final position.[8] Examples /kaše/ 'hard' (rec. Zelda G.), /šmone/ 'eight', /ze/ 'this' (rec. Dalia D.).

Non-native speakers, particularly native speakers of European languages (French German, Hungarian) as well as Arabic speakers, will use a tense vowel in all positions. Where the spelling has 'tsere', this pronunciation will be encouraged by the scholars in order to maintain in speech the distinction which formerly existed[9] between 'tsere' (a close tense vowel) and 'segol' (an open lax vowel).[10] English speakers tend to replace [ɛ] by English [æ] and to diphthongize the tense [e] to [ei].

---

[7] Only where spelling has final 'yod'. These endings may be represented as /ej/.

[8] Where spelling has final 'heh'.

[9] Gesenius 1910:46–47.

[10] Some discussion has centred around an attempt to distinguish /e/ and /ɛ/ as separate phonemes. A minimum pair offered has been /ben/ 'son' /bɛn/ 'son of', the latter being the construct state of the former. Although the first form is written with 'tsere' and the second with 'segol', soliciting from native speakers has demonstrated that the two forms today are absolute homophones. A greater difficulty is the pair /bɛn/ 'son' or 'son of' and /ben/ 'between'. The latter however is written with 'yod' and may be represented as /bɛjn/. Furthermore, many educated speakers will in fact make no distinction.

2.6. HEBREW VOWEL NO. 3 /a/

Hebrew vowel no. 3 /a/ is a fully open front vowel with open lip spreading to neutral lip position. Examples: /gam/ 'also', /ani/ 'I', /amami/ 'popular, primary (school)', /bagilboa/ 'on Mt. Gilboa', /mešuna/ 'strange' (rec. Nechama Ch.). There is a tendency in some speakers to pronounce a back vowel approaching [ɑ], e.g., [jerušalɑim] 'Jerusalem', particularly before a pharyngeal 'ayin', with speakers who pronounce the 'ayin'. Even with those who do not, the knowledge that the root contains an 'ayin' influences some speakers to pronounce [natɑti] 'I planted', reserving [natati] for 'I gave', which has no 'ayin'.[11]

2.7. HEBREW VOWEL NO. 4 /o/

Hebrew vowel no. 4 /o/ is a rounded back vowel between half-open and half-closed. The degree of lip rounding which varies with the speaker seems to be greater (closer) than that of cardinal vowel no. 6. It is a higher and more closely rounded vowel than the open English RP vowel in 'hot' or 'shop' and higher and more closely rounded even than the English vowel in 'short' or 'saw'. Yet the Hebrew vowel is lower than cardinal no. 7 and has less lip-rounding. Examples: /lavo/ 'to come', /tixon/ 'secondary school', /gadol/ 'large', (rec. Nechama Ch.); /šloša/ 'three', /šmonim/ 'eighty', (rec. David Sh.). R'uma Eldar, a principal announcer and news broadcaster on Kol Yisrael, invariably refers to that radio station as [koljisraʔel] with a very high closely rounded [o], exceptionally close to cardinal no. 7. In word final position, however, the /o/ does tend generally to close up, even sometimes to the extent of diphthongization, e.g., [zʔt] 'this', [jəmamʔt] 'days', but [po] 'here' (rec. Rabin). The 'hello' on the telephone is frequently [halou].

2.8. HEBREW VOWEL NO. 5 /u/

Hebrew vowel no. 5 /u/ is a fairly high back vowel with fairly close lip rounding though, being a lax vowel, it is far lower and more advanced than cardinal no. 8 and even than tense English vowel /u/. The Hebrew vowel has tongue and lip positions very close to the lax English vowel /u/ as in RP 'book'. Examples: /mul/ 'opposite', /nfuxa/ 'inflated', /raʔu/ 'they saw' (rec. Nava), /bidjuk/ 'exactly', /sipur/ 'story' (rec. Rachel D.). There seem to be no subsidiary members of this phoneme in E.I.H. English speakers of Hebrew tend to substitute a tense variety of /u/, a commonly heard 'English' pronunciation is [kibu:ts] for [kibuts] 'a collective farm'.

---

[11] I owe this pair to Shelomo Morag, who claims this as evidence of a separate /ɑ/ phoneme (see footnote 6). Recordings however show that the tendency to /ɑ/ is very restricted even before 'ayin. A recording of Yitshak Rabin, born in Jerusalem, shows free variation between [a] and [ɑ], even the word /lmaGase/ 'indeed', with 'ayin, is heard as [lmaase], not [lmɑase], but [haja] 'was', [hahavgazot] 'the shelling', [brera] 'alternative', [ela]—'but', but [pagazim] 'shells', also [maamacim] 'efforts'.

2.9. THE HEBREW *SHWA* /ə/

The Hebrew *shwa* /ə/ is essentially very short and unstressed. It is pronounced with the tongue and lips both in neutral position of rest similar to English non-final /ə/[12] as described by Gimson:[13] "a central vowel with neutral lip position, having tongue-raising between half-open and half-closed". Examples: /vəšmone/[14] 'and eight', /bəxolon/ 'in Holon' (rec. Dalia D.), /kəmora/ 'as a teacher' (rec. Dina G.).

In certain contexts, but not consistently, the tongue is raised to at least the half-closed position and advanced and lips spread somewhat, so that an [e]- or [ɪ]-like vowel is heard. This occurs, (a) before an immediately following vowel, e.g., /bəana-šim/ 'with people' (rec. Nechama Ch.), /tšaməot/ 'nine hundred' (rec. Dina G.); but parallel with these examples we have a normal mid-central pre-vocalic *shwa* in /vəotsma/ 'and power', and again /kəaraiot/ 'like lions' (both rec. Rabin); and (b) where the *shwa* is lengthened beyond its characteristic brevity, as for example in /və.../ 'and.... (rec. Dina G.) where the /ə/ is drawn out to /e.../ while the speaker is trying to make up her mind what to say next; and (c) when some speakers have a *shwa* so close to Hebrew vowel No. 2 /e/, as to be indistinguishable from it.[15]

2.9.1. *Functions of* shwa

Most of the examples in the previous paragraph illustrate the transition function of the *shwa*. /v/, /b/, /k/, /l/ are all bound morphemes meaning respectively 'and'; 'in' or 'with' or 'at' or 'on'; 'as' or 'like'; 'to'.

In the process of prefixation a consonant cluster is prevented by the intrusion of the *shwa* as a transition between the consonant prefix and the initial consonant of the word, the free morpheme to which it is attached. In rapid speech and particularly where the prospective consonant cluster formed consists of two consonants only, there will very frequently be no intrusion of transitional *shwa*. Thus /kəmora/ 'as a teacher' will be /kmora/, /b(ə)ʔelef/ or /bəelef/ 'in a thousand' will be /bəelef/ or /belef/. These are free phonetic variants having no linguistic significance.

2.9.2. *Alternation of* shwa *and* /a/

However the *shwa* or absence of it (zero) varies significantly (phonemically) with /a/ or /e/ in all cases after prefixed /v/, /b/, /k/, /l/. For example: /k(ə)mora/ ∼ /kamora/ 'as(like) *a* teacher' ∼ 'as (like) *the* teacher'; /b(ə)ʔelef/ ∼ /beʔelef/ 'in *a* thousand' ∼ 'in *the* thousand', e.g., /beʔelef harišon/ 'in the first thousand', where /ka/,

---

[12] Daniel Jones' [ə₁] rather than his [ə₂] or his [ə₃] which approaches [ʌ]. See Jones 1957.

[13] Gimson 1962:119.

[14] This form /vəšmone/ violates the textbook rule that /və/ → /u/ before an initial consonant cluster or an initial labial, but the form is well authenticated in the recordings (e.g. rec. David Sh. also has /šivim vəšmone/—'seventy-eight').

[15] Chaim Blanc's native speaker recorded in Blanc (1957) has both /və/ and /ve/ varying freely.

/ba/ etc., is the contraction of /k(ə)*ha/, /b(ə)*ha/ etc., /ha/ being the definite article 'the'.

The rules of Part II of the "Investigation" (see Preface) will state explicitly the regularity of the alternation /a/~/zero/ in the verbal forms, e.g., /šaxav/ 'he lay', /šaxva/ 'she lay', /katav/ 'he wrote', /katvu/ 'they wrote', where a base vowel /a/ is deleted as a result of the affixing of morphemes having certain phonetic shapes.

From the above description of the *shwa* as a 'transition' it will be clear that the Hebrew *shwa* will always be medial, never word-initial or word-final (the 'word' being taken to include prefixes and suffixes).

2.10. DIPHTHONGS

All five Hebrew vowels form vocal palatal glides by raising the tongue towards the *yod* position. These are all falling diphthongs, the first element being more prominent than the second. Examples: /talmidej/ 'pupils of', /axarej/ 'after', /elaj/ 'to me', /mictajnim/ 'excellent', /hajta/ 'she was' (rec. Oded B.Ch.). Most commonly these are word or morpheme final sequences, though several examples (not from the text) can be found in medial position: /lajla/ 'night', /habajta/ 'home', /cijru/ 'they drew'. Other examples (not from the text) are /safuj/ 'sane', /panuj/ 'vacant', /goj/ 'nation'.

2.10.1. Phonemic status of diphthongs

Although the glide sequences /ij, ej, aj, oj, uj/ qualify as diphthongs in that each forms 'a combination of full vowel with glide vowel', 'each is a syllabic element' in Hebrew (conditions laid down by Sweet and, in other terms, by both Heffner and Pike), nevertheless the morpheme structure of Hebrew requires that Hebrew diphthongs be not considered as monophonemic but as being made up of vowel plus *yod*. This will be clear if we examine every occurrence of diphthong in medial position. The two examples above will serve to demonstrate. /mictajnim/ 'excellent (m.pl.)' derives from /mictajen/ 'excellent (m. sing.)' by adding plural morpheme /im/ stressed. The previous final vowel /e/ of /mictajen/ loses stress and is deleted, yielding /mictaj-nim/. The three-consonant root is *cjn*, the base vowel pattern 'i...:é', which, when in-fixed, gives /cij:én/. Whereas in the singular the /j/ is clearly seen and heard as consonantal and the syllabic division clearly heard as /mic-ta-'jen/, with the movement of the stress in the plural, /mic-taj-'nim/ will be spoken with the altered syllabification indicated. This example from the text has the slight disadvantage of being complicated by the intrusion of the reflexive element /t/.

The example may be simplified if we choose a cognate non-reflexive verb /mca'jen/ 'indicates or singles out' (instead of /micta'jen/ 'excels, is outstanding'). The plural of /mca-'jen/ is /mcaj-'nim/ again with the second radical /j/ forming a diphthong with the preceding vowel, and the third radical /n/ beginning the heavy chest pulse producing the final heavy stress on the plural affix /'-im/.

That no claim can be made for monophonemic status for the diphthong can be shown by comparing the example just given with the word /mca-'nen/ 'cools', with its plural /mcan·'nim/, where the change in syllabification clearly maintains the VC sequence of Hebrew morpheme structure. We are not suggesting then that the medial sequence /aj/ functions any differently from /an/ within the structure. We are not claiming V status for the diphthong. It remains VC.

This disclaimer must be made to anticipate the objection of traditional grammar which writes a *shwa* in place of the deleted vowel in the plural /mic-ta-'jənim/, /mca-'jənim/ and divides the words into syllables as shown, with the sequence containing the shwa being included in one syllable with that containing the following full vowel.

The second example (from the text) of medial diphthong, /haj-ta/ 'she was', alternates with /ha-ja/ 'he was'. In this case the feminine suffix /ta/ stressed causes contraction of */ha-ja-ta/ to /haj-ta/. Other examples (not from the text):

pl.		sing.
oj-'nim	~	o-'jen 'hostile'
oj-'vim	~	o-'jev 'enemy'
xij-'vu	~	xi-'jev 'obliged'
xuj-'vu	~	xu-'jav 'were, was obliged'

2.10.2. Diphthong formed with bilabial velar glide

In some speakers (not recorded), a bilabial velar semivowel forms a diphthong after /u/ and before /a/, thus /'ruax/, /'luax/, /'duax/ 'wind', 'table or calendar', 'report', may become [ṙuwax], ['luwax], ['duwax]. One example appears in the recordings [lannuwax] 'to rest' (rec. Dalia Sh.).

3. CONSONANTS

3.0.1. General features of Hebrew consonants

Hebrew consonants are all egressive and pulmonic.

With the exception of two native and one borrowed 'foreign' nasal consonant, all consonants are oral, the soft palate being in raised position.

Obstruent pairs are distinguished by the feature of voice. (The exception to this is the fricative /š/ (voiceless only) and the affricate /c/ (voiceless only.).

3.0.2. Borrowed consonants

At the present time four borrowed consonantal segments should be considered as separate from the Hebrew system: /ŋ/ as in /baŋk/ 'bank'; /ž/ as in /želej/ 'jelly'; /č/ as in /čips/ 'chips'; /ǧ/ as in /ǧip/ 'jeep'. These are severely restricted and exist only in recent foreign borrowings. They will be mentioned in rather more detail in the section on nasals, fricatives and affricates respectively.

3.1. INVENTORY OF HEBREW CONSONANTS

Apart from these foreign borrowings, Hebrew has 17 phonetic consonantal segments. Of these, two are nasals, one bilabial /m/ and one alveolar /n/.

Examples: /gamru/ 'they finished' (rec. Shoshana G.) and /ani/ 'I' (rec. Shoshana G.): there is one affricate, a voiceless dental /c/, e.g., /cion/ 'Zion' (rec. Oded B.H.), one voiceless palato-alveolar fricative /š/ e.g., /šel/ 'of' (rec. Shoshana G.), and a lateral /l/ e.g., /šel/ 'of' (rec. Shosh. G.).

3.2. OBSTRUENTS

The remaining 12 consonantal segments form a 3×4 pattern:[1]

/p/	/b/	/k/	/g/	/t/	/d/
/f/	/v/	/x/	/r/	/s/	/z/

[1] By including the 'imported' phonemes, Chaim Blanc (in Blanc 1964) achieves a more symmetrical

Three plosive pairs, /p/, /b/; /k/, /g/; /t/, /d/, each pair corresponding to a pair of homorganic fricatives: /f/, /v/; /x/, /r/; /s/, /z/. The box enclosing the first three plosives, /p/ /b/ /k/, indicates phonemic identity with their corresponding fricatives, /f/ /v/ /x/, respectively.

3.2.1. Features of the plosive consonants

The set of Hebrew plosive consonants comprises seven members grouped in three pairs: /p, b/; /t, d/; /k, g/; plus a single glottal /ʔ/, the latter varying more or less freely with zero, 'more or less' since the glottal tends to appear initially in an intonation group, in intervocalic position or where special emphasis is expressed.

The members of the plosive series are distinguished from one another by point of articulation (bilabial, alveolar, velar) and by force of articulation (fortis, lenis). Presence or absence of voice and degree of aspiration are minor distinguishing features.

These distinctions are identical with those described by Gimson[2] for the English plosives. However aspiration plays a minor part in Hebrew probably due to the infrequent incidence of stress in rapid speech. The only examples we have in the corpus of fairly heavily aspirated plosives are in strongly emphatic position, e.g., [mas′phik] 'enough' (rec. Rivkah) or ['khen] 'yes' (rec. Esther O). In other cases, e.g., /kol kax ma′her/ 'so quickly' (rec. Esther O.), the first stress in the group is on the last syllable, or even in /histakalt biktovot lfi ha′daf/ 'did you look at the addresses on the sheet' (rec. Esther O), where /k/ carries a secondary static[3] stress in the group, neither plosive carries appreciable aspiration. It is significant that heavy aspiration or affrication of fortis plosives in Hebrew is considered by native speakers a sure sign of British or American origin.

The feature of VOICE must be considered as minor to that of FORCE in distinguishing homorganic plosives. As in English, voice is appreciably present in the Hebrew lenis plosive only in intervocalic position. Initially and finally there is very little (/p, b/ do not occur in word final position in Hebrew[4] except in 'foreign' words). Thus /toda′ti/ 'my thanks', is distinguished from /doda′ti/ 'my aunt' by the single fortis/lenis contrast. Examples from the text are /ze lo ba bəxešbon/ 'it's out of the question', (rec. Rivkah), where all /b/s are markedly lenis, yet with scarcely a trace of voice.

---

tabulation of consonants—a 4×4 system:

/p/ /b/   /t/ /d/   /č/ /š/   /k/ /x/
/f/ /v/   /s/ /z/   /ǧ/ /ž/   /g/ /r/

which leaves him only the affricate /c/ as a 'left-over'.

[2] Gimson (1962) and other authors have a fifth distinction—"length of preceding sounds" particularly vowels which in English are cut short by a following fortis consonant.

[3] The terminology used is that found in Kingdon (1958).

[4] The phonological rules will be stated in the "Phonology".

3.2.1.1. *The glottal stop*

The glottal stop in Hebrew derives phonologically from the voiceless glottal plosive /ʔ/ (*'alef*) as well as from the voiced pharyngeal consonant /ʕ/ (*'ayin*). More recently it also derives from a dropped /h/, a voiceless glottal continuant. However the recordings show that the glottal stop realization of these three separate phonemes is itself as often dropped as pronounced. In the examples from the text, Dina G. and Nechama Ch. seem to have the following rules: (a) omit the glottal in intervocalic position; (b) pronounce in initial position unless word forms a breath group with preceding word; (c) pronounce initially and intervocally for emphasis. Example from Nechama Ch.: /məʔod məod jafa/ 'very very beautiful', with glottal in first /məʔod/ but not in second. Yet Zelda G. has /məod məod/ 'very very', without any glottal (and without any emphasis). David D. is even more inconsistent and has few glottals even initially when unemphatic, though he claims that in front of his class (he is a teacher as well as a student) he makes a point of giving full value to the laryngeals and pharyngeal consonants, which he drops in his normal speech. Particularly interesting is Dalia D., whose parents speak Yemenite Arabic at home, yet who evinces the same lack of consistency in the production of laryngeals,[5] e.g., /baʔarec/ 'in Israel', but /belef tšamot/ 'in 1900' (instead of /bʔelef tsamʔot/; then /ʔarbaʔ im/ 'forty' and then /avarti/ 'I moved' (and not /ʔavarti/). Dalia Sh.' born in Casablanca,[6] also has few glottals even initially, e.g., /az/ 'well' (not /ʔaz/), /asaper/ 'I shall tell' (not /ʔasaper/). Once she has /ʔani/ 'I', and once /ani/ 'I' (without glottal). /kipa aduma/ 'Red-Riding Hood', but /ʔomnam/ 'however', /exad/ 'one', but /ʔaf al pi/ 'although'.

3.2.2. *Fricatives*

The set of Hebrew fricative consonants comprises eight members, six grouped in three pairs: /f, v/; /s, z/; and /x, r/; a single voiceless palato-alveolar /š/, a single voiceless glottal /h/, this latter varying more or less freely with /zero/ or /ʔ/.

The members of the series are distinguished from one another by point of articulation (labio-dental, alveolar, palato-alveolar, velar and glottal) and by force of articulation (fortis, lenis). The feature of voice must be considered as minor to that of force in distinguishing homorganic fricatives, voice being appreciably present in the Hebrew lenis fricative only in intervocalic position. Initially and finally the element

---

[5] Popular 'oriental' Hebrew is characterized by its marked pronunciation of pharyngeals. One Yemenite feature which is peculiar to Dalia D.'s Hebrew is a marked nasalization of vowels e.g., /temãn/ 'Yemen'.

[6] The fact of Dalia Sh.'s having been born in Casablanca is no grounds for surprise at her dropping initial laryngeals. I am indebted to Chaim Blanc for pointing out that this is in fact characteristic of Moroccan Arabic.

of voice is considerably reduced, e.g., /axšav/ 'now' (rec. Zelda G.), /larxov/ 'into the street' (rec. Naava K.).

3.2.2.1. The labio-dentals

The labio-dental fricatives are /f, v/, fortis voiceless and lenis voiced respectively.

/f/ appears in word initial position only in loan words, e.g., /film/ 'film', /fəlafel/ 'felafel', /fantasti/ 'fantastic', etc. /v/ is initial only in a dozen words: /vav/ 'hook', /vikuax/ 'argument', /vilon/ 'curtain', /veset/ 'menses', /vlad/ 'child, cub', /v (ə)ʔida/ 'conference', /vered/ 'a rose', /vitur/ 'concession', /vešet/ 'oesophagus', /vrid/ 'vein', /vatik/ 'old', /vadei/ 'assure'.[7] Besides these, /v/ is initial in the prefixed morpheme /v/ 'and'. This initial /v / alternates with /u/ where the following morpheme to which it is prefixed (a) begins with a labial consonant, e.g., /upitom/ 'and suddenly', instead of */və-pitom/; or (b) has *shwa* /ə/ as its first vowel, e.g., /uləagija/ 'and to get to . . .' (rec. Nechama Ch.) derived from */və-ləagija/.

Otherwise initially, these fricatives alternate with their cognate bilabial plosives,[8] /p, b/. Thus /paʔam/ 'time', but 'from time to time' will be /midei paʔam ləfaʔam/, /birex/ 'he blessed, greeted', but /ləvarex/ 'to bless to greet'.

3.2.2.2. Dentals

The dental fricatives are /s, z/, fortis voiceless and lenis voiced respectively. Point of articulation varies with the speaker from upper teeth to alveolar ridge, (even to lower ridge, with a not uncommon tendency to lisping, though this is considered defective). /s, z/ are not restricted as to distribution and appear initially, medially and finally.

3.2.2.3. Velars

The velar fricatives are /x, r/, fortis voiceless and lenis voiced respectively, In producing this pair, the back of the tongue is raised to the soft palate forming a trough with the rear rims of the tongue actually making contact with the palate while the uvular rests in the trough without vibrating. The voiced member of this pair, /r/, is sometimes trilled with the back of the tongue tapping rapidly against the soft palate. Both of these varieties are heard in rec. Dalia D. [baʔarets] 'in Israel', [betsefer][9] 'school', and yet in the same sentence [betsefer] 'school' and shortly after [axevRa] 'the company'. Most recordings however show a consistent fricative /r/ with the trill rare. Arabic speakers have a tongue-trilled apical /r/ which is recommended by official bodies (the radio).[10]

---

[7] These initial /v/ words derive from an earlier /w/.

[8] Explicit rules will be stated in the "Phonology".

[9] I have departed from IPA notation here and use [r] to represent fricative velar and [R] for trilled velar.

[10] Y. G. Gumpertz (1953) quotes Sa'adia Gaon (10th century) and other early grammarians to show that Hebrew had both alveolar and uvular /r/, the former following dental consonants.

5 1 2 2 4

Both /x/ and /r/ have unrestricted distribution, except that /x/ is never initial when it derives from the /k/ phoneme (see section 3.2.). In that case it will be realized as its homorganic plosive /k/ in initial position and /x/ only medially and finally.[11] Example: /katav/ 'he wrote', but /lixtov/ 'to write', or /mixtav/ 'letter'. This follows the same rule which alternates /f/ with /p/ (see section 3.2.2.1.). Initial /x/ will therefore invariably derive from a /ḥ/ phoneme which in Arabicized Hebrew is a strident glottal fricative with strong pharyngeal constriction, replaced in all positions by /x/ in E.I.H. The /ḥ/ is recommended by all official bodies and is widely used by radio announcers, but the recordings show not one /ḥ/ throughout, not even from speakers born in Arabic countries.[12]

3.2.2.4. Glottal

The breathed glottal fricative, /h/, occurs only in syllable initial prevocalic position and varies freely with /ʔ/ or /zero/. Thus we have the same speaker (rec. Rivka M.) beginning one sentence with /'hi/ 'it', and another with /'i/ 'it'. Medially in the sentence but word initially /ha'ʔir/ 'the town', and word medially, /vəha'ʔir/ 'and the town', and yet /airi'ja/ 'the town council' (not /hairi'ja/). Naava M. has /'ʔena/ 'hither', for /'hena/, and Fruma A. has /ma'er/ 'quickly', for /ma'her/. In these examples the position of stress is indicated to show that pronunciation or dropping of the /h/ is not dependent on stress.

There does seem to be a strong tendency to drop the initial /h/ of a second element in a group to create a kind of liaison with the first element, e.g., /tkufot is'toriot/ 'historical periods', /batei-avra'a/ 'rest houses', but many counter examples prevent us stating this as a rule, e.g., /al xof ha'jam/ 'at the sea shore'.

3.2.2.5. Voiceless palato-alveolar

The voiceless fortis palato-alveolar fricative /š/[13] is not different from the English consonant except for one common variety peculiar to young women. This has been noted and described by Chaim Blanc[14] as "prepalatal perhaps alveolar". The auditory effect is, in fact, almost that of a soft whistle, a hissing rather than a hushing sound, produced by advancing the front of the tongue to a pre-palatal position while the tip

---

[11] The rules will be stated explicitly in the "Phonology".

[12] Recordings made subsequent to the present study show a marked [ḥ] in speakers from Arab countries who immigrated to Israel AFTER completing primary school.

[13] 'Hissing' and 'hushing' fricatives and affricates are indicated by the following departures from IPA:

ʃ = š;   tʃ = č;   ʒ = ž;   dʒ = ǧ;   ts = c when representing the Hebrew affricate phoneme; ts = ts when representing two adjacent phonemes /t/+/s/.

[14] Blanc 1964: 138.

and blade make light contact with the alveolar ridge. Examples: /šnataim/ 'two years', /birušalaim/ 'in Jerusalem' (rec. Zehava C.); /šana šlišit/ 'a third year', /šimušit/ 'useful' (rec. Aviva S.), /xodeš/ 'month' (rec. Chaya T.).

This variety of /š/ exists in small children of both sexes and in young women in their teens and into their early twenties, when it disappears and is replaced by the more general palato-alveolar hushing /š/. A possible explanation for this peculiarity in some women has been offered by one of our informants. She suggests that some girls feel that this prolonging of a childish pronunciation makes them sound 'cute' —but that this can only be carried off up to a certain age.

3.2.2.6. Voiced palato-alveolar

A voiced palato-alveolar fricative /ž/ exists in foreign borrowings only, such as /ruž/ 'rouge', /žurnal/ 'journal', /garaž/ 'garage', /žele/ 'jelly', /miraž/ 'mirage' (aircraft), /kav mažino/ 'Maginot Line'.

3.2.3. Affricates

The only true affricate in Israeli Hebrew is a fortis, voiceless, dental /c/. It is formed by closing the air-stream by firm contact of tip of tongue against the upper teeth, while upper and lower teeth are clenched and then forcing the air out through and between the teeth. /c/ appears initially, medially and finally. Examples: /cura/ 'form', /joce/ 'he goes out', /erec/ 'country' (rec. Nechama).

3.2.3.1. /t-s/ sequence

A distinction must be drawn between the affricate /c/ and the sequence /t-s/, where two clearly separate morphemes coalesce. This may happen in any one of the following circumstances: (a) in a group where /t/ is final in the first word and /s/ initial in the second, e.g., /bet-sefer/ 'school', /bet-soar/ 'prison', where the first word /bet/ = 'house'; (b) where /t/ and /s/ are root consonants of the word and become immediately adjacent through the reduction or deletion of an intervening vowel, e.g., /tsisa/ 'fermentation, excitement', derived from the verb /tasas/; (c) where the nominalizing prefix /t/ is affixed to a word beginning with /s/, e.g., /tsumat-lev/ 'attention', derived from /t/ plus the verb /sim-lev/ 'to attend'.

An ambiguous pair (suggested by Chaim Blanc) is /huca/ 'he was thrown out', and /hutsa/ 'she was flown', from the roots /jc?/ and /tWs/ respectively.

3.2.3.2. Borrowed affricates and /t-š/ sequences

A fortis, voiced palato-alveolar affricate, /ǧ/, and its lenis, voiceless cognate /č/ exist in a small number of foreign borrowings only. Examples: /ǧungəl/ 'jungle'

/ǧuǧitsu/ 'jio-jitsu', /ǧip/ 'jeep', /čips/ 'chips', and /pančer/ 'puncture' or 'break-down'.

A distinction should be made between this borrowed affricate /č/ and the sequence /t-š/, which is common in Hebrew in words like /tša-esre/ 'nineteen', or /tša-meot/ 'nine hundred', where the first element /tša/, of the group is felt to be a contraction of /teša/ 'nine', (similar to what has been described in section 3.2.3.1.). Less obvious to a native speaker is the separateness of the /t/ as a nominalizing prefix in /tšuva/ 'answer', or /tšura/ 'gift', respectively from /t-šuv/ and /t-šur/. This sequence /tš/ might then be considered as a phonetic affricate.

/tr/ and /dr/ also form phonetic affricates in Hebrew although the morpheme structure of all Hebrew words in which they appear clearly demand that they be re-garded as composed of two separate segments, e.g., /truma/ 'contribution', derives from /taram/ 'he contributed', (consonantal root /trm/) where the nominalization involves deletion of the first base vowel /a/. Similarly /drom/ 'south (of)', (construct state), derives from /darom/ 'south' (absolute state), again with deletion of the first vowel. /tr/, /dr/ occur medially /litrom/ 'to contribute', /hidrim/ 'he went south', but not finally.

These limitations in distribution (which also apply to /tš/), together with the bi-phonemic function of these phonetic affricates, are sufficient to deny them full affricate status and to justify our statement in section 3.2.3. that /c/, which suffers none of these restrictions, is the only true Hebrew affricate.[15]

3.2.4. Nasals

Hebrew has two nasal consonants, a bilabial nasal, /m/, e.g., /gamru/ 'they finished' (rec. Shoshana G.) and an alveolar nasal, /n/, e.g., /ani/ 'I', (rec. Shoshana G.). Nasals occur initially, medially and finally.

3.2.4.1. Borrowed velar nasal

A nasal velar consonant /ŋ/ exists in recent loan words, e.g.,[16] /baŋk/ 'bank', /taŋk/ 'tank', /aŋglia/ 'England', /piŋ-poŋ/ 'ping-pong', /boiŋ/ 'Boeing', /gaŋgster/ 'gang-ster'.

In Hebrew words, the feeling that the segments /n/ and /g/ or /k/ form two of the three consonantal root elements of the word[17] is probably the reason for maintaining their separateness. All the same, there is a tendency with many speakers to assimila-tion of the two segments, though less so with new words created on the basis of the Hebrew roots. Compare /hangana/ 'intonation' and /mangina/ 'tune', both derived

---

[15] Similar considerations are stated for English by Gimson (1962) in selecting /tš/, dž/ as true English affricates and in excluding /ts/, /tr/, /dr/.

[16] Of these examples only /taŋk/ appears in the corpus, in the plural /taŋkim/ rec. Rabin).

[17] Morpheme structure rules will be formulated in the "Phonology".

from the root /ngn/. The first is a new coining, still a 'learned' word, the latter already well-worn and in popular use.

3.2.4.2. Velar nasal at word juncture

A purely phonetic /ŋ/ may occur at word juncture when final /n/ assimilates with initial /k/ or /g/, e.g., /eze min kufsa/ 'what kind of a box', may be heard as /eze miŋkufsa/, or /eze min gafrur/ 'what kind of match', may be heard as /eze miŋgafrur/.

3.2.4.3. Syllabicity in nasals

The nasals will never be syllabic (as in English button /bʌtn̩/) since a nasal will find itself in immediate proximity with a preceding consonant only as a result of the deletion of an intervening vowel and this deletion will take place only in case a suffix beginning with a vowel is added to a word, when this vowel will be the sonority peak of the affixed syllable and the nasal its initial consonant, e.g., /ma'tan/ 'giving, presentation', /mat'nat/ 'presentation of'. In common Arabic proper names which are referred to frequently in Hebrew, a syllabic /n̩/ or /m̩/ may appear in the word /ibn/, e.g., *Ibn Ezra*. More commonly however in foreign words, a final nasal following a consonant will give rise to the intrusion of a helping vowel, e.g., /film/ → /filim/.

3.2.5. Lateral

The Hebrew lateral /l/ is a voiced frictionless continuent. In all positions it has the resonance of what in English would be considered a 'clear' [l], that is, the resonance of a front vowel. Examples: /ləat-ləat/ 'little by little', /lirxovot/ 'to Rehovot', /gil/ 'age', /kol/ 'all', /aliti/ 'I immigrated', /itxalti/ 'I began', (rec. Zehava C.).

A certain type of 'darkening' of the /l/ in Hebrew is a sure give—away of the native English speaker.

3.2.6. Semi-vowels: yod

The Hebrew semi-vowel *yod* /j/ is a glide from a tongue position in the region of tense /i/. Lips are spread or rounded or neutral depending on the vowel following the *yod*, e.g., /jihje/ 'it will be', with spread lips before /i/, /e/, /aja/ 'it was', with neutral lip position before /a/, /jom/ 'day', or /jordim/ 'go down', /šijur/ 'lesson' (all rec. Rachel D.) with rounded lips before /o/, /u/. /j/, being the morpheme prefix of the third person masculine in the future tense, may be affixed to any verb and may immediately precede any first root consonant of the verb, e.g., /jsader/ 'he will arrange' /jlamed/ 'he will teach', /jkabel/ 'he will receive', etc. In rapid speech no 'helping' vowel is required after the *yod*.

This will be the case particularly when the group is preceded by a word ending in a vowel, e.g., /hu jsader/ 'he will arrange', /jona jlamed/ 'Jonah will teach'.

In more deliberate speech a *shwa* will act as a transition between the first two segments, e.g., /jəkabel/, /jəsader/.

The occurrence of /j/ before consonant is not restricted to verbs. /j/+C may form initial cluster in nouns, e.g., /jrušalaim/ 'Jerusalem', /jdid/ 'friend', /jdiot/[18] 'news'. /j/ in all these cases before a consonant should be considered as syllabic—in all cases phonetically and in its morphemic role, as functionally too.

The glide in /j/ may also be TOWARDS a tongue position in the region of /i/. This will be the case where the /j/ is preceded by any of the five Hebrew vowels /i/, /e/, /a/, /o/ or /u/. Examples: /ijej/ 'island of', /itonaj/ 'journalist', /goj/ 'nation', /panuj/ 'unoccupied'. The distance through which the tongue moves up and forward will vary in each case. In /ij/ the distance will be short though the final tongue position will be higher, almost entering the consonantal region, while in final /ej/ the distance will be very short and the auditory effect may be no more than a tensing of the /e/.

In /aj/ the distance will be longest though the final position of the tongue may be no higher than lax [i], the resultant final sequence being heard as a falling diphthong [ai]; similarly /oj/ and /uj/ are generally heard as diphthongs.

[18] Chaim Blanc (in Blanc 1960: 20) contrasts /jdiot/ 'news', which he writes /idiot/ with /idjot/ 'idiot', by indicating the difference in syllabification: the former he divides /i+di+ot/ and the latter /id+jot/.

4. STRESS

Stress is generally on the final syllable of the Hebrew word, less commonly on the penultimate, and rarely on the ante-penultimate.

4.1. FINAL

Examples of final stress are /ma′spik/ 'enough', /ne′lex/ 'let's go', /ax′šav/ 'now', /ma′kom/ 'place' (rec. Rivka G.).

4.2. PENULTIMATE—IN SEGHOLATE NOUNS

Penultimate stress will occur regularly in 'segholate' nouns[1] (see section 4.5.1.). Examples: /′sefer/ 'book', /′elef/ 'a thousand', (rec. Dina G.), /′mešek/ 'farm', /ɛrec/ 'country' (rec. Nehama Ch.).

4.2.1. With stressless suffix

Penultimate stress will occur regularly where the word ends in a stressless suffix, such as /-ti/ 'I', /-ta/ 'you', /-nu/ 'we', /-tem/, /-ten/[2] 'you' (m., f., plural), these being affixed to the verb in the past tense, e.g., /ha′laxti/ 'I went', /ha′laxnu/ 'we went', and also in the form /še′lanu/ 'our' or 'ours', and /a′naxnu/ 'we', or /o′tanu/ 'us', /i′tanu/ 'with us'.

4.2.2. In dual forms of nouns

Penultimate stress will occur regularly in the dual form element /aj/ of nouns. Examples: /šaa′tajim/ 'two hours', (rec. Rachel D.), /šińajim/ 'teeth', /e′najim/ 'eyes', /miška′fajim/ 'eye glasses', /of′najim/ 'bicycle', etc.

---

[1] So called because they received *seghol* [ɛ] as their second or "helping vowel" (Weingreen, 1939).
[2] /-tem/, /-ten/ appear in all standard grammars as stressed suffixes. In the Hebrew here described they are unstressed.

4.2.3. Names and places

It seems the rule with most speakers to stress penultimately those names of persons in common daily use and some place names. Thus in referring to one another the Israeli will stress penultimately /'avram/ 'Abraham', /'jicxak/ 'Isaac', /'jakov/ 'Jacob', /'sara/ 'Sarah', /'rivka/ 'Rebecca', /'raxel/ 'Rachel', /'lea/ 'Leah', /'moše/ 'Moses', /'aron/ 'Aaron', /'mirjam/ 'Miriam', /'juda/ 'Judah', etc. Yet in reading the Bible or referring to the Biblical characters they will stress the final syllable in each case: /av'ram/, /jic'xak/, etc.

In the case of place names we have /'xefa/—'Haifa', /petax 'tikva/ 'Petah Tikva' (rec. David Sh., who lives there), /re'xovot/ 'Rehovot', /'rišon lə'ci-on/ 'Rishon Letzion', /'tverja/ 'Tiberias', /na'tanja/ 'Nathania', all older towns, and of the newer /di'mona/ 'Dimona', /kirjat 'šmona/ 'Kiryat Shmonah'.

However the position of stress in place names is by no means fixed at this time; Tel-Aviv is stressed on its final syllable, Ashkelon /ašklon/ in one and the same recording is given once a final, once a penultimate stress by the same speaker (rec. Rivkah M., who lives there). The tendency generally seems to advance the stress of names, both of persons and of places, in the teeth of determined resistance on the part of the schools.

4.2.4. Foreign words

Foreign words will generally maintain their original stress even when a normally stressed Hebrew suffix is added, e.g., /pensi'onim/ 'pensions, boarding houses' (from the French *pen'sion* or German *Pen'sion*) (rec. Rivka M.), /uni'versita/ 'university' (rec. David D.), /geo'grafja/ 'geography' (rec. Rachel D.), /stu'dentim/ 'students' (rec. Shoshana G.). This is the case too where only part of the word is foreign, e.g., /pal'maxnik/ 'a member of the Palmach'. Here, the *nik* element is from Yiddish where it is invariably unstressed.

4.2.5. Final vowel plus /ax/

Words ending in vowel+/ax/ are stressed on that penultimate vowel, e.g., /'koax/ 'strength', /ta'puax/ 'apple', /'piax/ 'soot', /ləša'beax/ 'to praise'. This is the case frequently with words ending in vowel+/a/ where /a/ is not a morpheme suffix, e.g., /kol'noa/ 'cinema', /ga'rua/ 'inferior'; but this occurs only where /a/ is epenthetic. Example: /mac'ia/ 'he suggests', derives from /mcia/ʔ with epenthetic /a/ before final ʔ. /maci'a/ 'she suggests', derives from /mciʔ+'a/, the final /a/ being a morpheme suffix.

4.3. ANTEPENULTIMATE OR PENULTIMATE IN COMPOUNDS

Antepenultimate stress[3] or penultimate occurs in certain compound words: /'ezeš (e)hu/ 'some-or-other', /'mišehu/ 'someone', /'mašehu/—'something', /mi'kolma-

---

[3] Examples from Rosen (1956).

kom/ 'anyway', /al'kolpanim/ 'anyhow', /'kolbo/ 'receptacle', or store for assorted objects and goods, /'xarkax/ 'afterwards', /lif'nexen/ 'beforehand', /'bxolzot/ 'all the same', nevertheless. And numbers: /'xadasar/, /'šnemasar/, /'šlošasar/, /'šmonaasar/, /'šlošesre/, /'švaesre/, /'tšaesre/, /'šlošm(e)ot/, '11', '12', '13', '18', '13' (f.), '17', '19' (f.), '300'.

Wherever these words are broken down into their constituents and used as separate words, stress reverts to normal final position. So for example /mi'kolmakom/ 'anyhow', but /mi'kol ma'kom/ 'from every place', /al'kolpanim/ 'anyhow', but /al'kol pa'nim/ 'on every face'.[4]

4.4. PAIRS IN WHICH STRESS IS SOLE CONTRASTING FEATURE

A short list of pairs of words may be drawn up in which position of stress is the only distinguishing significant feature.

/'boker/ 'morning'	/bo'ker/ 'cowboy, cattle raiser'
/'bira/ 'beer'	/bir'a/ 'capital city'
/'ima/ 'Mother'	/i'ma/ 'her mother'
/'dvora/ 'Deborah'	/dvo'ra/ 'wasp'
/r'xovot/ 'Rehovot'	/rxo'vot/ 'streets'
/'oto/ 'automobile'	/o'to/ 'him or it'
/'kama/ 'she rose'	/ka'ma/ 'she rises'
/'šara/ 'she sang'	/ša'ra/ 'she sings'

[4] The Chomsky-Halle principle of the "transformational cycle" suggested for prediction of stress in English word sequences and word compounds seems to apply here. See Chomsky and Halle 1968. Chomsky and Halle first assign stress to the smallest immediate constituents of the word or word sequence, then re-apply their rules in a second cycle to the next bracketing of constituents. On this second cycle, a rule (which could not apply on first cycle) would weaken a final stress on a bracketing labelled as some CATEGORY (e.g., noun, verb, etc.) while maintaining the final stress in a bracketing labelled as some SEQUENCE (e.g., noun phrase, prepositional phrase etc.). Example:

$$\text{baby sitter} - \left\{(^1\text{baby})_N + (^1\text{sitter})_N\right\}_N \quad \left\{^1\text{baby } ^3\text{sitter}\right\}_N$$

$$\text{baby sister} - \left\{(^1\text{baby})_{Adj} + (^1\text{sister})_N\right\}_{NP} \quad \left\{^2\text{baby } ^1\text{sister}\right\}_{NP}$$

$$\text{Similarly with} \quad \left\{(\text{toy})_N + (\text{cupboard})_N\right\}_N \quad \text{'a cupboard for toys'}$$

$$\text{as against} \quad \left\{(\text{toy})_{Adj} + (\text{cupboard})_N\right\}_{NP} \quad \begin{array}{l}\text{'a cupboard}\\ \text{which is a toy'.}\end{array}$$

Further rules reduce the stress on the second element of the N to tertiary and the first element of the NP only to secondary. Determination of the position of stress from constituent structure is borne out by Philip Lieberman's experiments (Liebermann 1967) which confirm that "perceived linguistic stress is often a secondary manifestation of the derived constituent structure. The listener mentally 'computes' the linguistic stress by means of the derived constituent structure of the utterance. He determines the derived constituent structure by means of the words of the sentence, by the breath-group divisions through 'disjuncture' (where the constituent structure of the phrase is ambiguous)." 'Disjuncture' is defined by Liebermann as "intervals between the words".

4.5. INFORMAL STATEMENT OF RULES FOR STRESS

To sum up this section on stress we might attempt to state the situation informally.

4.5.1. Stress inherent in second vowel

The structure of the Hebrew word comprises two discontinuous morphemes, a consonantal root and a vocalic element consisting of two vowels, or one vowel and zero. Stress in Hebrew may be considered as an intrinsic feature of the second vowel, or, where there is only one vowel in the vocalic element (as in the case of segholate nouns —see section 4.2.), then stress is a feature of that vowel. In the first example, in section 4.4., where both words are indigenous Hebrew, the difference in stress position is predictable from the underlying structure of the two words, the first derives from /bkr+o/ (or /u/) and is therefore stressed on the sole base vowel /o/, the /e/ being epenthetic or as Gesenius and others call it—a "helping" vowel. The derivation of the second is /bkr+a...a/ which nominalizes by changing to /o...é/ to generate "actor" form.

4.5.2. List of suffixes carrying characteristic stress

Certain morpheme suffixes carry characteristic stress. When any of these are affixed to a word, the word stress will be on that suffix. These suffixes are: /-i/ 'my, me', '-xa, ex/ 'your, you (m.f. sing.)',[5] /-o/ 'his, him', /-a/ 'her' (see footnote 5), /-'enu/ tour, us', /-xem/, /-xen/ 'your, you (m.f. pl.)', /-am/, /-an/ 'their, them /m.f.)', /-im/ (m.pl.), /-ot/ (f.pl.).

Verbal suffixes: /-a/ third person singular feminine; /-i/ second person singular feminine; /-u/ second and third person plural.

Nominal endings: /-a/, /-on/, /-an/, /-ut/, /it/, /-aj/.

Adjectival suffixes: /-i/, /-it/.

4.5.3. Stress loss on second vowel

In such cases where stress moves to the suffix, the vowel previously accented will lose its stress.

Examples with unstressed suffix are: /micta'eret/ 'am sorry (f.)', /hi'xanti/ 'I prepared' (rec. Shoshana G.).

Examples with stressed suffix are: /maki'ra/ 'I know (f.)', /axo'ti/ 'my sister', /mitlab'šim/ 'get dressed (pl.)', /ašli'šit/ 'the third (f.)', (rec. Rachel D.).

Exceptions are: /jəru'šalmi/ 'Jerusalem (adj.)', /jəru'šalmim/ 'Jerusalemites'.

---

[5] When preceded by a vowel these suffixes lose their stress which moves back to that preceding vowel, e.g., /dvaŕexa/, /dvaŕajix/—'your words', /dvaŕe(h)a/ 'her words', /e'lexa/ 'to you'.

5. INTONATION

The phonology described in this part of the study (and accounted for in a forth-coming volume[1]) does not include, in any detail, the intonation of Hebrew. A comprehensive description of Hebrew intonation patterns reflecting all the attitudes and emotions which may accompany utterances would require a larger and more varied set of recordings than those we have made here. All that has been attempted here was to solicit and record 'cold', unemotional, unemphatic monologues, such as newscasts read by Reuma Eldar of Kol Yisrael, the Jerusalem radio station, a press conference held by Yitshak Rabin, Israeli Chief of General Staff at the end of 1967, student autobiographies in a nutshell spoken impromptu in front of a microphone and two matter-of-fact conversations between students before a concealed microphone. From these an attempt has been made to determine the basic intonation patterns of such 'cold' sentences. An additional procedure used, rather artificial perhaps, was to solicit sentences of the various types—statements, questions of various kinds, commands—from the same students who had acted as informants for the main part of this work.

The terminology and notation used in this section will be that suggested by Roger Kingdon.[2]

5.1. KINETIC TONES

As a general rule it was found that alterations in pitch occur on stressed syllables. A stressed syllable on which a change of pitch occurs is said to carry a KINETIC tone. It is the kinetic tones which give colour to utterances, which, without them, would be said on a monotone. The more rapid the speech, the longer the breath group, the fewer (or the weaker) the stresses within the group, the longer the sequence of monotones. An example of a typically long breath group is the following from a newscast:

/...ʔašer jaxrĭa/ ʔim ˈlagoliṣtim jihˌje ḳvar ˌʔata ṛov baʔaseˌfa halʔumit šel carəˈfat/ [...which will determine whether the Gaullists will already have a majority in the French National Assembly.] (Rec. R. Eldar).

---

[1] Chayen, "Phonology", forthcoming. See the Preface.
[2] Kingdon 1958.

The same speaker, slowing the pace of her newsreading, announces:

/ʔatem maaziňim/ ləšiḍur haḥadašot bə₁kol jisra͵ʔel/jərušaìajim[You are listening to a news broadcast on Kol Yisrael, Jerusalem.] (Rec. R. Eldar).

Slashes in this section indicate breath group boundaries. As indicated by these examples a kinetic tone occurs on the last stressed syllable of each breath group. Other stressed syllables have either a high or low static pitch.

5.2. FALLING TONES IN DECLARATIVE SENTENCES

The kinetic tones falling on the last stressed syllable of each breath group are NUCLEAR tones in that their function is to give added meaning to the words. In the two examples given above, the nuclear tone of the final breath group in each utterance is a falling tone and indicates finality of the utterance. Sentences of the 'statement' type end in this way.

Unstressed syllables following a falling nuclear tone are spoken on a low pitch. Example: /...k̀orsika/ (rec. R. Eldar).

5.3. 'wh' QUESTIONS

'Wh' questions use this same nuclear falling tone. Examples: /maˈtaj atˈbaa eˈlaj ˈkcat lə saˈxek im ajˊeled/ 'When are you going to come to me to play a bit with the baby?' (rec. Minda B.-I.). /ˈefo aàxta/ 'Where did you get to?' (rec. Michael G.).

5.4. COMMANDS AND EXCLAMATIONS

Commands and exclamations use this same falling tone. Examples: /ˈal tociu ˋhege/ 'Don't speak a word' (rec. Naava K.), /boˋena/ 'Come here' (rec. Michael G.), /ˈsgor et haˋdelet/ 'Shut the door' (rec. Naomi Ch.).

5.5. YES/NO QUESTIONS

Yes/no questions have a rising tone on their last stressed syllable. Examples: /t jo₁daat ḳama hi rǫca/ 'D'you know how much she wants?' (rec. Rivka G.). /biˈkarta beharcaˊa/ 'Did you attend the lecture?' (rec. Fruma A.).1. Any unstressed syllable following the rising final stressed continues the rise in pitch. Example: /hajita bauni͵yersita/ 'Were you at the University?'

5.6. RISING TONES

Breath groups which are non-final in the utterance use a rising nuclear tone to signal the fact. This may occur at the end of a subordinate clause preceding a main clause or vice versa, or in the case of slower speech where the utterance is broken up into short breath groups. A good example of this latter is the deliberate delivery of the following sentence:

/kox'otenu hitkad'mu/vehi'giju/be'kecev ma'hir/tox havka'a/šel maara'xot/kfi šecijanti mə-vuca'rot/... 'toxk'de ni'hul/kravmat'mid/'akša'ni /'mə₁nuh'al ja'fe 'aljə'de kol haməfak'dim / bə'xol hagza'rot / 'aljə'de kol haxaja'lim / šegil'u / ce'ruf mug'ba / šel haka'ra / jə'xolet /vəra'mati'mun₁ gvohà /. [Our forces advanced, rapidly penetrating the fortified lines, which I referred to, fighting all the while, and without respite, stubborn battles, ably conducted by all commanders in all sectors, and by all soldiers, who showed a superb combination of sense of duty, ability, and high standard of training.] (Rec. Y. Rabin).

5.7. FALLING-RISING TONES

A falling-rising tone is often used instead of the rising tone particularly on the nuclear syllable of a breath-group which is non-final in the utterance. Examples: /ani mačia/še.../ 'I suggest that...' (rec. Rivka G.), /bə'ʔize/ mitxolel ata maʔavak mišpati / sviv gora₁ lo šel hamošav / ašer jaxřia /₁im.../ 'In this island a legal struggle is going on concerning the fate of this colony, which (struggle) will determine wheth-er...' (rec. R. Eldar).

It will be noted that the falling-rising tone may be distributed over two or more words, e.g., /bə'ʔi₁ze/. In addition to the falling-rising tone a 'rise-fall-rise' is illustrated on the word /mišpati/. This is a further variation of the plain rising tone and occurs frequently in comm n speech.

5.8. OTHER POSSIBILITIES

The above description of certain tones as characteristic 'cold' realization of certain sentence types does not imply the exclusion of the possibility of other tones being used, but the difference will probably mark some additional meaning or colouring not carried by what we have called the characteristic tones.

5.9. MARKED AND UNMARKED INTONATION

Our observations of the characteristic tones of Hebrew accord with Lieberman's view of types of intonation of languages in general as being of two basic kinds: unmarked (falling) and marked (rising), or with Armstrong and Ward's view of

English intonation adopted by Daniel Jones[3] as consisting of two tunes, Tune 1 (falling) and Tune 2 (rising). Lieberman cites instrumental analyses of ten languages which confirm that the 'normal' breath-group ends on a falling tone:[4] "The normal breath-groups of all languages are similar in that they end with a falling fundamental frequency contour."

This is also the case in Hebrew, the neutral or unmarked tone being the falling tone, while the rising tone, where used, is the sole marker of (a) interrogation and (b) non-finality.

[3] Jones 1957.
[4] Lieberman 1968.

APPENDIX

EXTRACTS FROM THE RECORDINGS

These extracts are in broad transcription. Only samples of intonation are given.

1. Dina G., born in Israel of Russian parents, lives in a kibbutz, served two years in the Army.

no'lati bə'ʔelef 'tšameot ʔarba'im vəxa'meš bəkfar ʿsa͵ba. ke'van še... ʔimi ʔv'da kəmo͵ɾa ʔa'laxti kvar bgil cair bi'karti ba'gan biḳarti bo šə͵loša'nim 've... bəgil 'šeš halaxti ləbetašefer. la͵mati bəveta͵sefer bar iḷan bəkfar ʿsa'ba e... bakita ͵hej cta͵rafti l tnuat͵noar bnei a͵ḳiya ve... 'šam bi'liti et rov zma'ni axa'rei hacoho'raim axarei alimu dim. ba... m ʔe... ləbetasefer tixon lamadti gamken bəota ʔir bekfar saba ze betsefer tixon xadaš šeikimu lamaxzor šelanu. naxnu aji:nu amaxzor arišon šenigaš ləbagrut bəbet sefer atixon aze betsefer tixon morešet e... horai ...horeinu hikimu oto mišum še lo racu šeanaxnu nisa lilmod bəir axeret vəalken ikimu bet sefer tixon dati bəkfar saba. ʔe... kšaiti bkita əšišit itxalti ladrix bətnua. idraxti šnataim və-neeneiti məod məavoda. hi gam hosifa li arbei vəani zoxeret b(ə)tkufa azot kəaxad atkufot ajafot bxajaj... tom alimudim hitgajasti lənaxal. biliti šnataim bəšnei məšakim. bəšana ašnija ləšeruti ʔavadti kəmora bəvetsefer šafir. betsefer azori šafir əjad encurim. ʔe gam šana zo ajta axad ašanim ajafot. neeneiti minavoda və irgašti šeani mitpataxat ba. laaxarmiken laaxar ašixrur ʔe... xazarti abajta və bəota šana itxalti lilmod bəuniversita ani lomedet ləšon ivrit vəsifrut ivrit... ani gara karega bəkfar darom.

Translation:

I was born in 1945 in Kfar Saba. Since my mother worked as a teacher I went... I attended kindergarten already at an early age. I attended kindergarten for three years and... at the age of six I started school. I went to Bar Ilan School in Kfar Saba... In grade 5 I joined the 'Bnei Akiva' youth movement and... there I spent most of my time after school in the afternoons. In the... er... secondary school I also studied in the same town in Kfar Saba—that's a new secondary school that was founded for our year. We were the first year to take the matriculation exam at that school, 'Moreshet' secondary school. My parents... our parents founded that school because they didn't want us to travel to another town to study and so they set up a religious secondary school in Kfar Saba. When I was in the Sixth Form I became a leader in the movement. I was an instructor for two years and I enjoyed the work very much. It gave me quite a lot, too, and I remember that period as one of the best in my life. When I left school I joined the *Nachal* [pioneering youth brigade] and spent two years in two settlements. In my second year of service I worked as a teacher in Shafir school, Shafir regional school near Ein Tsurim. That year, too, was one of the finest in my life. I enjoyed the work and felt that it gave me maturity. After that, after demobilization... I went home and the same year began studying at the University. I'm doing Hebrew language and literature... Just now I'm living in Kfar Darom...

2. Nehama Ch., born in Israel of Hebrew- and Yiddish-speaking parents, lives in Tel Aviv, served two years in the Army.

...be'xofeš aga'dol e... bexofeš bəmešex xod'šaim ajiti betijul beẋuclaạrec ʔe... və... aja 'dei məan'jen lavo meerec dai provincij'alit kmo sela‚ṇu uləa‚gija lnjujok agdol'a upiṭom ʔa'nii... ʔaxat bə tox olam gadol mameš niv'lati šam vaja nexmad lirʔot šešam 'kol aḍam hu a'dam bif'nei acṁo hu ‚lo taḷuj ḳol ḳax beanašim axer'im. mamaš boletet sam auvda sel axofeš 1 əmašal bimjuxad li ze balat barakevet ataxtit kəšenixnasti ləšam kolʔadam ʔasa šam... ʔitnaeg šam bəcura axeret bəcura məjuxedet məšuna muzara vəafaxad lo istakel alav lo zelobixlal mašax et tsumat lev kəšenixnas lə šam kamcan lə mašal az kol axad taram t trumato vəmijad xazar laiton šelo bəota acura axi... šigratit ʔaxi regila. šam lirot adam nixnas larakevet ataxtit kore et a iton jored bətaxana šelo lo mistakel bixlal vəjocei axuca... tov njujok lo bəecem kol kax jafa hair ajoter jafa bəenai i: šikago ʔir amerikanit tipusit mə'ʔod məod jafa.

Translation:

...in the long vacation... in the vacation for two months I went on a trip abroad... and it was quite interesting, coming from a fairly provincial country like ours to arrive in big New York and suddenly I... was swallowed up there... one in the midst of a great world. And it was good to see that there everyone is a person in his own right; he's not so dependent on other people. The fact of freedom stands out a mile, for example, it struck me particularly in the underground railway. When I went down there, every person did... behaved there in a different way, in his special way, peculiar, strange and no one looked at his neighbour, wasn't the least bit interested. When a beggar got in, for example, everyone gave him something and straightaway got back to his newspaper in the same... routine, ordinary way. There... to see a man get into the underground railway, read his newspaper, get off at his station, not look at anybody and go on out... Well, New York isn't actually so beautiful. A more beautiful town in my eyes is Chicago, a typical American town—very, very beautiful...

3. David D., born in Israel of Polish parents, lives in Tel Aviv, served $2\frac{1}{2}$ years in the Army.

... 'ʔaf al pi šekaašer haxaverim 'kan šomə'im ˌoˌti, ani xoˌšev, mzahim oti bəkaˌlut kəca'bar ʔaval afʔalpi xen lifaṃimʔani joḏea ˌše si'galti ləac'mi bəofen məlaxuti kol minei ə... diḇur kcat 'šoˌne meḥacaba'rim, kloˌmar ˌʔaf al ˌpi šeaˌni ˌgam xo'tef 'lo 'paam hava'rot šo'not 'vəmavlija, aval l(ə)gabei hagijat.. məsujaṃim hagiˌja šeˌli šonˌa ləmašal bxol ofen bvet aṡefer. atalmidim lo zaxu lišmoa mimeni af paam lo xet v lo ajin ela tamid rak het vəʔajin vəše ani mədaber az kaše lomar šeze bolet kol kax ə... ləgabei hareš kamuvan še af al pi še jaxolti ani mamšix lagot reš imbalit...

Translation:

...even though when my classmates here listen to me speak, I believe they can easily identify me as a native speaker, all the same sometimes I know that I've adopted artificially all kinds of... speech, a bit different from the *tsabarim* [native Israelis], that is to say that although I also swallow various syllables and not infrequently, yet as regards the pronunciation of...certain...(sounds?), my pronunciation is different. For example, at least at school my pupils have never had the 'privilege' of hearing from me... neither [xet] nor [ajin], but always only [ḥet] and [ʔajin], and when I speak, it's difficult to say that it's so noticeable... As far as the *resh* is concerned, of course although I could, I always pronounce a *uvula resh*...

4. Shoshana G., born in Israel of Hungarian parents, lives in Tel Aviv, served two years in the Army.

... ni ˌdafka xaˌšavti ʔal ˌʔezešehi ˌba'aja šehi uˌlai aktu ˌʔalit po ləgabei 'kama ana-šim bxolofen i lo aktualit bidjuk ləga'bai ela ləgabei'anašim šeani maki'ra. zot abaja šel anaˌšim šegamru at uni'ver'sita və axˌšav niš ʔa'ru məxusˌrei avo'da. ze bee'met axad advarim šeani nitˌkal'ti bahem etṃol kšeni karati bəmaʔ riɣˌˌmoˌda~ʔa... maʔa'mar še'bo məˌsa'prim al moda~ʔot šemapilim anašim bap̂ax... macijim lahem avoḏot vəˌal jəḏe 'kax hem gam məvakšim mejem, ˌḳesef tmurat ze və'aljadei'kax mapi'lim ani'šim ba'pax. ani jodaat al kama studentim afilu šebeemet hitpatu laze vemekevan šehem axšav gamru vəlo nišara avoda bišvilam ʔiš ʔeno doʔeg lahem kajom afilu ʔiš eno jodea šehem mxusrei avoda ki en lahem lean li fnot...

Translation:

...Actually I thought of some problem which maybe concerns some of the people here, at least it doesn't actually concern me but people that I know. It's the problem of people who finished University and are left without work. That's really one of the things I've come across, yesterday when I read an advertisement in *Ma'ariv*—an article where they tell of advertisements which got people into trouble... they offer them jobs and at the same time ask them for money for it and so get them into trouble. I even know of some students who were fooled that way and since they've just finished and there's no work left for them, nobody worries about them today, no one even knows they're unemployed, since they've nobody to apply to...

5. Oded B., born in Israel of Hebrew-speaking parents, served 2½ years in the Army.

... zekaˈra bəaxad mibatei aˈsefer bərišon ləˈcion. talmidei bet aˈseˌfer aju joˈcim midei ˈjom bjo$_m$o ləsfat ajam ˈšam aˈju misaxaǩim. bəota ˈkitˋa ˌkiṭa ˌxet aju šnei ˈtalmiḏim aˈxim tˌəoˌmim šm̥uˈel və daˈvid ˋšmam aˈju atalmiˈdim amictajˈnim bakiˇta aˈju asportaˈim aˈmictajˈnim. lo kara paʔam šedavid isig et šmuel o šešmuel isig et david gam bəcijunim bamivxanim aja davar jom exad bəotam məsaxakim hineem roim al axad agvaot omed naʔar umitbonen bahem.

Translation:

It happened in one of the schools in Rishon Letsion. The school-children used to go to the sea-shore every day to play. In the same class, grade eight, there were two pupils, twin brothers, Samuel and David were their names. They were the best pupils in the class and outstanding at sport. More than once it would happen that David would beat Samuel or that Samuel would beat David—also in examinations. It happened one day while they were playing that on one of the dunes they saw a boy standing watching them...

6. Dalia D., born in Israel of Yemenite parents, lives in Holon near Tel Aviv.

noˈlati baˋʔarec ˌbelef tšamot ʔarbaʔim vəšm̥one. noˈlati bəxoˌvlon ləhorim jcei teˇman... txalnu lmod betsefer...e...xofši ʔad kta daled... um kita he avarti l bet sefer dati bet sefer jšurun mišam himšaxti bioto kivun ləbetsefer javne ə...e...mišam avarti ləbar ilan kevan še jitaxen še ze... pəxot o joter...

Translation:

I was born in Israel in 1948. I was born in Holon of parents who came from the Yemen. We began to study in a non-religious school till grade 4, and in grade 5 I transferred to a religious school, 'Yeshurun' school; from there I continued in the same direction to 'Yavne' school...er...um...from there I went on to 'Bar Ilan' since I suppose that's...more or less...

7. Zelda G. born in Russia of Polish and Rumanian parents, went to kindergarten in Israel, lives at Lod.

ˈješ li ʔǎxot ʔ: ... ˈdei mvuġeret šelomed axšav bətiˠxon vəbə šminit axšav vəovedet kaše məod kdei l... i mitkoˈnenet lebxiṇot vəani mkaˈva šəi tacˈliax. ˌješ li gaṇ ˌax kátan šenimca bagan və...m...m̥əod nexmad. aˈni ohevet lišˈmoa kšeu m(ə)daber kəšehu məsaˈper et ˈkol axavaˈjot šelo min aġan. ani gam ohevet ləsaper lo sipuṛim al... maxšefot u məod məod mitrageš mejem um sipurim al kol minei zeivim o ai anašim raim vətamid u maftiax li še jitnakem bəkol aanašim araim...

Translation:

I've a sister... quite old, who's now at secondary school and in the eighth form and working very hard to... she's preparing for her exams and I hope she'll succeed. I've also a small brother who goes to kindergarten and... he's very nice. I like te listen to him talking and telling about all his experiences in kindergarten. And I liko to tell him stories about...about witches. He gets all excited about them and about stories of all kinds of wolves and bad men and he always promises me that he'll take revenge on all the bad men.

8. Dalia Sh., born in Morocco (Casablanca), came to Israel at the age of five, served two years in the Army.

ˌšmi dalja š... ani loumedet lašon ivrit vəarayit məsajemet hašaṇa mkava lagešet ləbxinot bsof šaṇa. ani nəsu ʔa ješ li štei jəladot ktaṇot ləaxat korim ... v lašnija korim giḷat bnot šana vəxeici v šnataim v xeici beintaim maspika kcat lilṃod kcat ltapel bahem. bšana haba ani mkava kcat lanṇuwax və ləhakdiš joter zman l jlaḍot ˈˈim kamuvan ani aspik lagešet ləbxinot bsof asaṅa. ajalda agdola šeli ohevet lišmoa šnei sipuṛim, eexad kipa aduṃa kamuvan, vəsipur ašeṇi šilgiˈja vəšivat a gamadˈim. ješ la afilu sfaṛim ˌomˌnam ˌlo joˈdaat liḳro aḍajin. af al pi še ješ šita xadaˈša ... kmo ˌše šaˌmati. [The rising intonation at the end of sentences is typical of this sort of monologue.]

Translation:

My name's Dalia Sh. ... I'm studying Hebrew and Arabic in my last year. I hope to take my finals at the end of the year. I'm married and have two small girls, one called D... and the other G... one and a half years old and two and a half years old. Meanwhile I manage to study a little and to look after them a little. Next year I hope to have a bit of a rest and give more time to the children providing of course that I manage to take my exams at the end of the year... My elder girl likes listening to two stories, one is Red Riding Hood of course and the other story is Snow White and the Seven Dwarfs. She even has books, although she can't read yet, even though there's a new system—as I've heard...

9. Zehava Ts., born in Morocco, came to Israel when she was two years old.

noladti bəmoroko vəaliti arca bəgil šnataim. avarnu lirxovot šam lamadti bəvetsefer
jəsodi ... lamadti birušalaim kaavor arba šanim kšegamarti itxalti laavod bašdod
btor mora... anii mlamed bbetsefer ramban ze haja bet sefer harišon bəašdod hadati
vəgam halodati beecem haja bəhatxala eze crif katan. bekita axad lamdu kol hatalmi-
dim. ləat ləat habetsefer hitpateax vəaxšav ješ bo esrim kitot kimat kol kita mxupelet
umšulešet. talmidim olim xadašim ruban me... jocei cfon afrika kama mehodu
paras aval harov kaxa mecfon afrika... kulam talmidim benonijim, ješ kama kašim
meod ki kaše lahem pašut lhitaklem baarec. ašdod acma bixlal lo kalta klum arec...
hi od ir tipusit mixuclaarec hasafa šešam mduberet rak carfatit lo šomʔim ivrit hi
mamaš nišeret ʔir metoceret xuc.

Translation:

I was born in Morocco and immigrated to Israel at the age of two. We moved to Reho-
vot where I went to primary school... I studied in Jerusalem. After four years, when
I finished I began working in Ashdod as a teacher... I teach at Ramban school.
That was the first religious school in Ashdod—actually the first school of any kind.
At first it was just a little hut. All the pupils learned in one class room. Little by little
the school developed and now it has twenty classes, each grade double or triple.
The pupils are mainly new immigrants from—emigrants from North Africa, some from
India, Persia, but most from North Africa... all average pupils, but there are some
very difficult ones as it's very difficult for them simply to acclimatize. Ashdod itself
...... is still a typical overseas town. The language spoken there is only French,
you don't hear any Hebrew. It's really remained a 'foreign-made' town.

10. Esther O., born in Israel of German and Hungarian parents, lives in Ramat Gan.
Rivkah G., born in Israel of German parents, lives in Tel Aviv.

(dialogue recorded in Jerusalem where the two students are flat-hunting)

E.   kama u roce
R.   u roce meavəesrim aval ašerutim hem ləmala
E.   az ze bixlal lo məcia
R.   az tire ani macia šenelex lə...šetiri et ze
E.   ken
R.   nelex lirot et lea ... ex efšar l(ə)špia al C... efšar l... im amxir
E.   ken kdai ldaber ita
R.   ken... axavera šeli... ajiti ecla kama pamim vəaiti ecla gam axšav i lo ajta
      babait aval jitaxen še bešaot ejle i tihje ... ajiti kodem...
E.   histakalt biktovot lfi hadaf šehem xilku

R.   lo lfi adaf . . . raʔ iti. . . cilcalti ləkama mkomot. . . ze haja saxur kfar.

E.   kol kax maher

R.   lo ze ktovot jəšanot, mamaš jəšanot. . . az . . . zehu . . . . . . ješ od makom
     exad. . .

E.   axšav po birxov aze ješ dira axad šeaxšav ani šomaat šedodati halxa. . .

R.   dirat studentim

E.   zot dira šnei xadarim. ovrim xeder mitox xeder aval ze lo nora bišvil štenu. . .
     axad at bexeder ani bəxeder. ze jaxol lijot nifla. . .

R.   aval gam məxirim niflaim kanire

E.   zeu. kanire še im dodati halxa lirot et ze, ze məxirim lo kol kax niflaim.

R.   ani lo crixa luksus kaze lihjot ləvad baxeder.

E.   lo ze šəela nagid im ze mataim lirot dira

R.   lo. mea lirot ləxodeš ani lo jxola lšalem

E.   vənagid mea šmonim

R.   lo—ani lo xoševet. at məvina im ajiti roca lagur ləvad ze lo aja expat li aval
     ani lo roca ləšalem vani lo crixa et adavar aze. lo expat li lagur štaim en li
     akesef lagur kol kax tov. . . lo kidai li en li amacpun laasot et ze . . . ajiti
     muxana šivʔim.

Translation:

E.   How much does he want?

R.   He wants a hundred and twenty but the conveniences are upstairs.

E.   Then that's no bargain at all.

R.   Look here then. . . I suggest we go and. . . you go and see it.

E.   Right.

R.   Let's go and see Lea. . . if there's any way of influencing C. . . . about the price.

E.   Yes, it's worth talking to her.

R.   Yes. . . at my friend's . . . I was round at her place several times and I was over
     there just now. She wasn't at home but maybe round about now she'll be home. . .
     I was there earlier. . .

E.   Did you look at the addresses on the sheet they distributed?

R.   Not on the sheet. . . I saw. . . I phoned a number of places. . . already rented.

E.   So quickly.

R.   No, they're old addresses, really old. . . that's it. . . There's one other place. . .

E.   Now, here in this street there's a flat I've just heard about. My aunt went. . .

R.   A student flat?

E.   It's a two-room flat—one room leads into the other—but for us two it's not
     so bad. . . you in one room and me in the other. That could be wonderful. . .

R.   And wonderful prices too, I expect.

E.   That's it. But apparently if my aunt went to look at it, the price can't be too bad.

R.   I don't need such luxury to have a room to myself.

E.   No. It's just a question of... say if it's 200 lira... the flat...
R.   No. A hundred lira a month... I can't pay that.
E.   And say 180.
R.   No. I don't think so. You understand if I wanted to live by myself, I shouldn't mind, but I don't want to pay and I don't need it. I don't mind living two together—I don't have the money to live so well—it's not worthwhile—I don't have the conscience for that... I'd be ready to pay seventy.

REFERENCES

Bachi, R.
 1956 *Statistical Analysis of the Revival of Hebrew in Israel* (Scripta Hierosolymitana III) (Magnes Press, Hebrew University, Jerusalem).
Blanc, Chaim
 1953 "Studies in North Palestinian Arabic", *Israel Oriental Society* IV (Jerusalem).
 1957 "Passage of Spoken Israeli Hebrew", *Leshonenu* 21 (Jerusalem).
 1960 *Intensive Spoken Israeli Hebrew, Book I* (English Language Services, Washington, D.C.).
 1964 "Israeli Hebrew Texts", *Studies in Egyptology and Linguistics in Honour of J. Polotsky* (Jerusalem).
Catford, J. C.
 (n.d.) "A New Description of English Phonology, and Its Use in the Teaching of Pronunciation", mimeographed.
Ferguson, W.
 1961 *Damascus Arabic* (Center for Applied Linguistics, Washington, D.C.).
Gesenius, W.
 1910 *Hebrew Grammar*, ed. A. E. Cowley, 2nd English edition (Clarendon Press, Oxford).
Gimson, A. C.
 1962 *An Introduction to the Pronunciation of English* (Arnold, London).
Greenberg, J. H.
 1950 "The Patterning of Root Morphemes in Semitic", *Word* 2 (New York).
Gumpertz, Y. G.
 1953 *Mivta'ei Sfatenu, Studies in Historical Phonetics of the Hebrew Language* (Mosad Harav Kook, Jerusalem).
Heffner, R.
 1950 *General Phonetics* (University of Wisconsin Press, Madison).
Hockett, C. F.
 1955 *A Manual of Phonology (= International Journal of American Linguistics, Memoir II)* (Waverly Press, Baltimore).
Jakobson, R., C. G. M. Fant and M. Halle
 1963 *Preliminaries to Speech Analysis* (M.I.T. Press, Cambridge, Mass.).
Jakobson R. and M. Halle
 1956 *Fundamentals of Language (Janua Linguarum 1)* (Mouton, The Hague).
Jones, D.
 1957 *An Outline of English Phonetics*, 8th edition (Heffer, Cambridge).
Kingdon, R.
 1958 *Groundwork of English Intonation* (Longman, London).
Levenston, E.
 1965 "A 'Scale and Category' Description of the Syntax of Israeli Hebrew", unpublished thesis (University of London).
Lieberman, P.
 1967 *Intonation, Perception and Language (= M.I.T. Research Monograph No. 38)* (M.I.T. Press, Cambridge, Mass.).

Mitchell, T. F.
  1958 *Introduction to Egyptian Colloquial Arabic* (Oxford University Press, London).
  1962 *Colloquial Arabic* (English Universities Press, London).
Pike, K.
  1943 *Phonetics* (University of Michigan Press, Ann Arbor).
Rosen, Ch.
  1956 *Ha'ivrit Shelanu* (Am Oved, Tel-Aviv).
Weingreen, J.
  1939 *A Practical Grammar for Classical Hebrew* (Clarendon Press, Oxford).
Yelin, D.
  1945 *History of the Development of Hebrew Grammar* (Trust for the Publication of the Works of D. Yelin, Jerusalem).

INDEX